Mapping the Sands

Mapping the Sands
poems by Geraldine Zetzel

Mayapple Press 2010

© Copyright 2010 by Geraldine Zetzel

Published by   MAYAPPLE PRESS
              408 N. Lincoln St.
              Bay City, MI 48708
              www.mayapplepress.com

ISBN 978-0932412-85-0

ACKNOWLEDGMENTS

A number of these poems have previously been published, some in different form, in the collection *A Wider Giving*, Ed. Sondra Zeidenstein (Chicory Blue Press), and in two chapbooks: *Near Enough to Hear the Words* (Pudding House Publications) and *With Both Hands* (Finishing Line Press).

I would like to thank the editors of various journals and publications in which versions of some poems have previously appeared, including *The Comstock Review*, *Cumberland Poetry Review*, *Crazy Quilt*, *The HILR Review*, *The Radcliffe Quarterly*, *Stone Country*, *Rhino*, and *The Worcester Review*.

My thanks to the members of the poetry seminars I have been part of at Radcliffe and Lesley University, as well as to those fellow-poets with whom I have met in informal workshops over the years. Their thoughtful reading and critique of my works-in-progress have made all the difference.

I am deeply grateful to all my teachers, especially Suzanne K. Berger and the late Kinereth Gensler. Special gratitude to Sondra Zeidenstein and to Kathleen Aguero for their invaluable help in putting together the early versions of the manuscript. Thanks to those later readers, Suzanne Berger, Susan Donnelly, and Fred Marchant, who helped me refine and complete the work.

To my dear family and friends: I am so thankful to every one of you for your encouragement throughout this project. Each of you has helped in your own particular way to bring this book into being.

Cover photo by Brian Jones. Cover designed by Judith Kerman. Book designed and typeset by Amee Schmidt with titles in Candara Italic and text in Californian FB. Author photo courtesy of Tesi Kohlenberg.

Contents

I

In February	5
The Goat	6
Brother Dog	7
Packing	8
Fur	10
A Visit to Munich, 1937	11
Hall Closet	12
The Family Room	13
Playing with Fire	14
The Canyon, 1945	15
Burning the Journals	17

II

Loom Song	21
Field Guide to the Birds	22
Waiting	23
Grief Is Another Country	24
Snapshot, 1963	26
Night Song, Winter	27
Anniversary	28
Fishing, 1972	29
Late Marriage	30
Night Light	31
Take This...	32
Kiss	34
Presence	35

III

Morning	39
Nectar	40
Green	41
Juice	42
Scenario	43
Swimmers	44

Together	45
Lincoln Park Zoo	46
Ode to the Porcupine	47
Traveling...	49

IV

Half a Cloak	53
Bad News...	54
Compassion	55
Imagining the Muse	57
The Sign	58
The Prince Who Married a Frog	60
Prospero, Departing	62
Miranda, Waking	63
Mt. Fuji Between the Waves	
off the Coast of Kanagawa	64
Carmelina	66
Still Life	68
Joy	69

1

In February

What wouldn't I give to live
inside that yellow kitchen

where an old deal table
sits like a dowager queen

two green pears all she requires.
Smooth as courtiers, they bow

to each other, bellies swelling.
And yellow tulips in a brown jar

speak softly into their creaking
sleeves, *Close your eyes. Listen...*

The Goat

Before I know I am human,
the goat nips bread from my hand,
his eye a sly black diamond
set slantwise in a yellow sun.

Before I take to the ways of words
I understand: ears can twitch in code,
hooves drum signals on the grass,
nostrils telegraph urgent news.

Before the protocol of spoons and forks,
I learn the sideways flick of jaws
neat-lipping green alfalfa,
strong teeth crunching the blossoms.

Why must I walk, block after boring block,
while his kind wheel on stiletto legs,
butt heads and caper out the gate,
tails flashing freedom?

Why must I wear stiff leggings
and itchy mittens, not a smooth coat,
its speckled pelt draped snug
to the shape of my bones?

Soaped and talcum-powdered,
dosed with Maltine and put to bed,
I long for the heady smells of manure,
rank straw and pee and milk.

I lick the skin of my wrist,
waiting to dream of the Goat-King—
his wicked horns and the way
his rough tongue savors my fingers' salt.

Brother Dog

My parents buy him on an impulse—
a cute pup in a pet-shop window.
They name him *Algernon*
and he goes through it all with me:
the divorce, the peregrinations,
one constant presence in my childhood.
On him I practice tyrannies
learned from the grown-ups: teach him
Beg and *Speak*, enforce obedience
with a spank. Shaming him
for non-existent crimes,
to see him droop and tremble.

Left to sit at the dinner table
until I have cleaned my plate,
I sneak him stringy bits of liver.
Mouthing the nasty morsels,
he spits out on the rug
what even he can't swallow.
After his bath, escaping the towel,
he races around the house, ecstatic—
pink skin shining through his wet pelt,
that funny freckled sack
bobbing between his hind legs.

Some nights, I sneak him into bed
to sleep beside me, a hairy
baby brother. I like to watch
his paws twitch, his piebald lips
draw back in a grin as he dreams;
I like to see the intricate landscape inside
the flap of his ear. Within that skull,
a sleep full of new tennis balls,
enemy bulldogs, a world
without names. No irregular verbs,
no lies, no posture lessons.

Packing

It always begins some weeks ahead,
the ritual of Going Abroad: starts with
a heaviness like before a thunder-storm.
The making of lists, the setting up

of trunks and suitcases in the spare room.
Then drifts of white tissue paper,
clothing laid out on chairs and beds,
pairs of shoes in ranks on the rug.

Layer by layer over many days
like an archeological dig in reverse
comes the packing itself. Heavy things
first: shoes encased in cloth bags,

winter coats and jackets, then
dresses and blouses folded
just so, tissue laid into each crease.
Underwear, scarves and gloves

bedded down in satin lingerie-cases,
and finally the most delicate:
the evening gowns—silken, shining—
wrapped and smoothed into place,

making sure that everything
emerges at the other side of the world
perfectly, as if just folded and boxed
by a deft salesgirl at Bonwit Teller's.

The dog and I stay out of the way,
watching in dread while the stuff of life
as we know it goes into suitcases
with metal corners and a steamer trunk

the size of an icebox, with fat brass locks
that swivel and clack into place
and a red Cunard Line sticker that says,
"*NOT WANTED ON VOYAGE.*"

Fur

Out of its shoebox coffin
and tissue-paper shroud
this legacy: one strip of mink
backed with dark-brown satin.
The pelt is soft, thick
as the bodies of old ladies
(*oh gentle flesh encased in whale-bone,*
feet bound in alligator-skin,
sweet brows winged and crowned
with the feathers of jungle birds!)

Lifting to my face this collar
saved from some last good winter coat,
instead of animal I inhale
a smell familiar as a chime:
woman... This creamy under-down,
the brown guard-hairs fragrant
with all the years
those little bodies lay tame
around some powdered neck.
Only the longing
remains, like the acrid thread
of musk that coils in at the window,
summer nights. And you waken
to stare down at the garden, asleep
under its quilt of street-light.
The air is rank with the smell
of raccoon. They grunt and dig
for grubs in the lawn, scuffle
high in the trees. The cries
of their love-making slice
through the city's distant rumble,
the tide of their bodies' heat
rises, pressing against
your shivering skin.

A Visit to Munich, 1937

Into the sunlight they march,
the soldiers in their jackboots,

and the band thumps gaily
while people stand by smiling

and little girls like me wave
flags. But Hilda, my nanny,

and her brother do not wave:
their faces go still and fixed

like bird-dogs that spot something
moving in the underbrush but

don't know yet what it is. After that
they take us to a famous beer-hall.

We sit at long trestle tables
among large men in Bavarian dress

who drink from big steins. It is hot.
Hilda's young cousin Anton and I,

allowed to share a beer, get sleepy
and silly. Hilda, shy with happiness,

sits close to her brother. There was singing,
I remember, and red banners hanging

from every rafter. And a white disc
at each flag's center, where the hooked

black crosses spun on and on
like gears getting ready to turn

the wheels of endless trains.

Hall Closet

The raincoats and galoshes. The Harris tweed and the silk duster. Umbrellas large and small ready for a rainy day. And the family skeleton: waterproof, mothproof, foolproof, fireproof. Invisible to the naked eye: everyone knows it but nobody names it. The children are well trained: when they reach in for their jackets, they know to push it quietly aside. At all times perfectly well-behaved, it glides obligingly out of the way.

Hangers have a way of understanding these matters. They know their place. The peach satin proud to hold up Madam's fur wrap with its delicate dangling paws. The jittery little cheap ones from the cleaners whispering into their sleeves. The matched set, covered in flowered chintz, reserved for guests. All of them in turn deferring to the smooth bulk of those broad-shouldered males, heavy maple, polished as brass, his accomplices.

Swaying among themselves, discreet as butlers, they never tell but never forget. His Chesterfield with its velvet collar. Carnation boutonniere pinned to the lapel. Smell of tobacco and *eau de Cologne*. White silk scarf. Deep in the pockets, a pair of pigskin gloves. The key to the opera singer's studio. The skeleton key.

The Family Room

That battlefield, bare
except for the ping-pong table
where she and her new stepfather
duel in dead earnest each night after supper—
she wordlessly driving her shots
into his continual volley of jokes
about women and Jews.
Their only witnesses the water heater
mumbling behind its screen,
the sprung sofa that smells of dog—

against whose stained tartan cover
late one Saturday her brother's friend,
home on leave from the Navy,
abruptly pins her down
with a heavy predatory kiss.
Her first—that rite she'd longed for,
that passage into a new land.

Stiff with shame, she waits it out,
her body locked, a Pandora's box
too dangerous to open,
at the very bottom of which
she imagines Desire
like the tiny prize you find
inside the box of Cracker Jack.

Playing with Fire

You know what will happen, they warned
when we were little. Meaning terrible things
like wetting the bed, or worse—like
something out of *Struwwelpeter*
where Paulinchen plays with the matches
when her parents go out to dinner
(although, the cats remind her,
das ist verboten).

But how to resist the hot drops
of wax that drip down dinner candles
while the grownups linger maddeningly
over coffee?—That searing wondrous
heat as you smear each fingertip
with molten wax, then peel it off.
The delicate caps then with their faint
transparent whorls, secret code
of your identity...

Wyoming summers,
we learned to swear horribly,
carry a stash of kitchen matches
to jiggle like coins in our Levi pockets.
The kind you could strike anywhere—
zip against boot-soles, floorboards,
pop against the copper rivets of jeans
or scrape top-speed across the seat
of the pants. (So many ways
to drive the grownups crazy...)
Heroes among us were the ones
who dared flick the blue match-head
wickedly across the thumbnail
(hands cupping the imaginary
cigarette—eyes squinting hard
under a beat-up Stetson), who suffered
the sulphur burning their fingers
and carried about them for hours
the delicious smell of *Danger, danger*...

The Canyon, 1945

Five kids—wartime ranch hands
let off for a few days' rest—
we go camping in Clark's Fork Canyon.
The Shoshone runs muddy and loud
from the year's late ice-melt.
Charlie and Jan, our best anglers,
casting, casting in long graceful arcs
for hours, but the trout never rise.
We survive on tinned ham, coffee
and bread, scare each other silly,
nights, with stories of rogue bears,
odd noises in the dark.

It must have been August 5, 1945.
Just about when they were briefing
the pilot and wheeling "Little Boy"
into the belly of the *Enola Gay*.

Giddy with hunger, the last day,
we struggle back out of the canyon
and wait by the side of the road
for the truck to come pick us up.
We sprawl in the shade and talk
about food. On the way back
to the ranch, the foreman tells us
the news they'd heard the night before—
speaking those words no one
had known till then: *atomic bomb,
mushroom cloud, Hiroshima.*

Unreal, the words, unreal
that the sun just goes on
stroking as usual the flanks
of the familiar mountains, that the tufts
of Indian Paintbrush keep on waving
scarlet in every ditch.

Not until later, not
until much later, when I see
the first images—shriveled husks
of bodies, blast-shadows
of bodies on walls—do I even
begin to understand. But what
did we ever understand?
That a whole city can be obliterated
in half an hour? That a river
can burst into flames?

They say a weed called *Panic Grass*
sprouted in the ruins a few weeks
after the blast, spreading green as acid
everywhere between the dead buildings.
Forgive us. By then we were busy
cutting alfalfa in the upper field,
raking it up before the next storm
could spoil the hay.

Burning the Journals

The puny flame   plays along the sheaf
of pages close-packed   as peony leaves
nibbles at the rim   refusing

to eat the past   I poke the truant
bead of fire   it flares up at last
a shaky purgatorial blaze

Sentences wrinkle   phrases curl
the ink burns with a bitter smell
words shrivel into threads of smoke

Long afterwards a secret click
and rustle keeps on   something unfinished
still moving   in the cinders

An old story   I want to lean
closer   want to lay my cheek
in the warm lap   of those ashes

A story that goes on asking
old questions   the way if you've lived
for a time in a cabin   beside some river

the rhythm of it talks on   in your sleep
flutters through your veins   for years

Loom Song

I have woven this carpet
out of the crumbs dropped from my plate

the drops of wine and coffee spilled
the stories I wanted you to hear

all the years you have been gone.
I have threaded the shuttle over

and over across the weft,
battening down each strand

to make the pattern: osprey
and fish, river and moon. And yet

it refuses to be complete:
each blue thread still looking

for its place, each red seeking
a shade to lie down beside.

Field Guide to the Birds

for Arthur Kohlenberg, 1924-1970

That June morning in the country,
our first year at the new house,
you went out one time at dawn
with your new binoculars
and Peterson's Guide in your pocket—
you who grew up in a city apartment
in the Bronx, where birds were either
pigeons or sparrows. Learning by the book
the way you'd already taught yourself
to make a cheese soufflé, mend
the window-screens, sail a boat.

You came back to wake me
apologetic, urgent: *You've got
to come—there's a tree
full of the most amazing birds—
they're not in the book...*
Leaning over me, you smelled
like grass clippings and morning,
your chinos soaking wet with dew.

I threw on my clothes
and we ran together back up the road
afraid they might have flown.
But there they were—
the big elm alive with them,
glittering like a school of fish.
Diving and jostling and whistling
by the hundreds, their bodies brilliant
with iridescent spots: a huge flock
of Common Starlings...
An army of promises, a host
shining purple and green
and golden in the morning sun.

Waiting

At 3 a.m. in the hospital room,
the silence buzzes like high-tension wires
as you watch the careful breathing in and out.

Or in the terminal, that stoic posture
as you watch the word *Delayed*
blink mindlessly on the monitor.

And when the doctor points at the X-ray,
noting the thing only a trained eye can see,
the seed of death in a cloud of cells, it is the same:

just a cloud at the beginning, a muttering
beyond the horizon. Only a probability.
You refuse to be afraid: *It won't happen to us...*

And by then of course it's already too late
for anything but the waiting. Too late to stock up
on batteries or bottled water, and in any case

the whole thing is unbelievable, isn't it?
With the sunlight falling on the trim lawn,
the white curtains lifting gently in the breeze.

Yet it will come, although we're unable
to imagine it. And it will end, in time.
After the hurricane has blown through,

the indifferent sun will shine. How to imagine it?
All that howling, the house shaking, about to split—
then only the acrid smell of green wood, broken.

Grief Is Another Country

Because I can imagine—just—your hand
touching this paper, I can hope
someone may receive this message.

The Country
After these six months,
the strangeness only grows.
Of course, the season changed.
I had been warned,
but nothing really prepares you for such cold.
At first I thought I'd understood
how it all fits together: climate, landscape,
figures in the foreground giving proportion.
But now the patterns more and more elude me,
maps don't contain the logic.
One is easily lost, and lost again
at turnings that had seemed familiar.
Landscapes change, or else my sense
of how things connect is altered. And then
they tell time differently here.
It seems I am always either too early,
too late, too distant or too close.

The People
Curious at first, eager to help,
now bland and friendly, they come and go
as if this house were theirs.
The habit of touching hands and smiling
—of which I wrote you—is not to be interpreted
quite the way I thought at first.
Yes, they mean well. But something else is meant.
At times you have the sense of being watched,
like some odd animal or child.
And it isn't clear what they expect.

The Language
There is nothing now I cannot express.
Words and their rhythms come easily to the tongue.
The syntax is delightfully regular. Still,
a kind of hunger haunts me—
for richness, maybe, or depth.
So much significance remains unsaid.
You wonder if the natives
speaking to one another
use a different dialect.

Daily Life
The house they gave me is large.
A certain shabbiness prevails
and there is that smell in the hallways,
odd but not unpleasant, like old tobacco.
Things leak or creak. I would get them fixed
if it were clear what is the landlord's business
and what is mine. Mealtimes are brief.
Although the food is palatable
I often feel a sickness much like hunger.
Work keeps me busy. I'm told I do it well.

I do it well. But ask them back there
to state again the purpose of this mission.
It grows less clear after so many months
why I am here. What is the meaning of my task?
How long shall I be prepared to stay?
The messages I get are so obscure.
Tell those in charge to write more plainly.
Tell them I will do my best.
      And try once more to find the books
I asked for. In exile you forget so much.
Faces begin to blur...
I will not sign this: my name
in this language has a different meaning.

Snapshot, 1963

He leans against the rim
of the catboat's cockpit,
reclining as at a feast.
The tiller pillows one elbow,
the other arm lies
draped along the rail.
Long fingers loosely hold
the slack of the line.

His mouth curves upwards
—that archaic smile
full of light and secrets
you see on the carved faces
of Olympic winners
or those Etruscan couples
propped side by side, at ease
on their marble sarcophagi.

Each June the old sailboat,
spars newly varnished,
slips into the bay again.
Sailing alone, I'll lean
my shoulder-blades against
the smooth curve of the coaming
and feel the wind press
its hard palms against my neck.

Night Song, Winter

I was alone   so I turned on more lights
I was dry   so I watered the plants

The leaves exhale   a whisper of green
Time to lock up— did you turn down the heat?

I make some tea   so the sheets will be kind
The hours wander by   blind as old cats

Swimming before bed   we laughed like thieves
I remember your hand   on the skin of my belly

Anniversary

I asked the calendar for an explanation—
  all it said was, *Later...*

I asked each one of the clocks in turn—
  they only answered, *Wait...*

Was it full moon, as now, the night you died?
  Did the high tide greet you as you went?

You used to say I had good cheekbones;
  no hand now touches my face

The lap of the river offers comfort,
  but still carries off whatever will float

The wind in the oak keeps on clearing its throat
  as though it had something important to say

Objects survive us, have lives of their own:
  the attic is full of dishes and books

Where is the man who washed up after supper,
  who lay reading late on the window seat?

Fishing, 1972

There we are, on a sandbar
in the middle of the Roaring Fork
somewhere north of Aspen
breathless from the altitude—
but game, oh yes, game—up to the point
where I fall behind and he gasps,
Wait! Stay here! Bob and the guide
plunging ahead in search of that fabled spot
a fishing-hole where enormous Rainbows
are said to lurk...
                  And he stumbles off
after the guys, borrowed waders flapping.
Leaves me stranded midstream.
*Big doctor—passionate come-lately
fly-fisherman, hell-bent on keeping up
with the boys, the goyim.* Never mind
our honeyed morning in the hotel bed,
the Mozart concert at the Festival,
lazy window-shopping on Galena Street.
*What makes me think I can marry
this middle-aged boy?*

Here turns out to be an alder thicket,
wilderness all around, the ice-melt river's roar
drowning out all hope of a human voice.
I hunker down on a willow log and contemplate
mosquitoes. Bob's wife had the sense
to stay back at the lodge, but I
—fearless Girl Scout and Good Sport—
had to cowgirl along, didn't I? Had to show
him I'm not that Park Avenue princess
he imagines. So here I sit and shred
rotten bark between my fingers, considering
if it would be smart to eat my sandwich now
or better to save it for later.
                          Wondering
if and when my prince will come, and how will he—
clueless as he is about directions even in the city—
ever find this sliver of riverbank again?

Late Marriage

for Lou Zetzel, 1911-1993

Old hands at loving, our bodies come together,
bumping along in a language they've come to know.
Parsing familiar grammar, the parts of each other,
syntax can get confusing. (*How does this go?*
Whose knee belongs where?) But bodies talk it over,
make sense. Mind-sense is harder work: we think
we're in step, then fall apart as we discover
a wrong turn taken, something out of sync.
Resident aliens in each other's cities, with queer
accents we'll never completely lose. And you
are a country I'll never know—near, so near...
But there are no visas. I watch your face in the blue
glare of the T.V. screen. A wave of fright:
Who is this stranger? Then strangeness becomes delight.

Night Light

Beside your craggy, sleeping face
the face of the electric clock
shines a wakeful eye.

Your cheek lies slack
as an old napkin, its folds
outlined by a rim of light.

Your forehead's bony hill
glows, the skin tight-drawn
to the mold of the skull.

Mouth half-open, lips dry,
you are drinking in the night
with each deep sigh.

In the mirror across the room,
this light repeats itself—
like a lantern deep in the woods

some woman has set in a window.
Waiting up late, wrapped
in an old quilt, she watches

the glow spilling onto the dry leaves,
how it pools like fine snow,
settles quietly everywhere.

And here in this room too it sifts down
onto your wallet and hairbrush,
your folded handkerchief.

Each night this snowfall arrives,
unseen. In the morning it's gone.
No one will ever know.

On the dresser, your watch will lie ticking.
Wallet, hairbrush will be dry. Your face
cool as linen in the pale of day.

Take This...

When you drag your left foot
across the kitchen floor
with a noise like a horseshoe crab
hauling itself over rocks,
I want to give you back your stride—
the solace of muscles performing
their unremarkable daily work.

And when you wake dazed, eyes blank
as a trapped cat's in the glare
of headlights, I want to give you back
everything you've lost—time and meaning
—a rush of reality, hot and sweet,
strong as your steaming mug of black China tea.

Or I could begin, and would,
by grafting my skin—here, where it's brown
and fine as watered silk—
to mend the roughened map
on the back of your hands. But that won't
change the way your fingers
shake as you try to sign your name.

No more than all my hoarded words
or this poem itself will restore
to your tongue those names
it mumbles through sleep to find.

> *The name of your teacher was Castle*
> *the name of your sister, Rachel*
> *and the river where you caught*
>   *your biggest trout,*
> *the North Fork of the Shoshone.*

Take all these, then. And take my rage
—its hidden hook and barb,
its intricate, deceiving feathers—
splice it to yours.
                    The way, by the pond,
last week, while I steadied the tip of the rod
you managed with infinite patience
to splice a dry fly onto the nylon leader:
one turn, then two more
around the filament,
up through the slippery eye of the loop,
then the final quick pull
to secure the knot.

Kiss

Nothing else exists for them—
not the boy rounding up
the jittery shopping carts,
not the hot mothers with their skeins
of trailing children

—these two kissing
in the parking lot at Lees' Market.
He lanky and bearded
stooping down to meet
her upturned face, she arching up
to be reached.

See: even their blue-jean knees,
their hips, are kissing now—
might be *Goodbye* or *Sorry*,
might be *Missed you*,
or maybe a sudden avalanche
of heat that just can't wait...

Their time to embrace, mine
to be reminded of the stubble
scraping my cheek,
the salty taste of shared breath
and that surge coursing
like honey through the body.

Presence

Today
after the beach
I came back to this high bright room
the northwest wind rattling the windows
and knocking the tethered dinghies
against the docks
and lay down on one of the sofas
my skin hot and tight from the sun
and slept in the belief
that someone was sitting
on the other side of the room
there in the blue armchair
reading the paper
waiting but not in any hurry
watching from time to time
my sleeping face and the breath
going about its business in and out of my body
and when I woke up there was a presence
as of someone just gone out of the room
for a moment

Morning

Days open this way:
a shout of wind

and two limbs of the elm
outside the window

striding slantwise along
into the sun's tide

like Johnny Appleseed
legging it over the blue

Or they open silently:
dream-doors sliding apart

in a house where light arrives
to bless each lintel

as somewhere deep in woods
an unseen pond

now takes the entire sky
gravely into its arms

Nectar

A mower charges across the park,
in its wake the pungent smell
of onion grass. And I am back
dawdling home from school
at the vacant lot, that corner
before the brick houses
with tidy lawns and clipped hedges
begin their march down our street.

A no-man's-land of mounds and thickets,
old cellar-hole, one twisted persimmon tree—
a secret territory where I root up
with fingernails the bulbs of the wild onion,
their bitter taste and the sour tang
of sorrel leaves my antidote
against the stodge of suppertime,
my vaccine against the clink
of soup spoons, tyranny of napkins.

Climbing through that sumac jungle,
I'd crawl under the wild grape's
ropey vines to taste that bead of nectar
drawn out from the honeysuckle.
Living off the land, like Mowgli's lost sister
or the stolen child kept by the gypsies.

Green

That spring, Lina the cook made Italy
into a new map for us—all green—
as the crop of fresh peas slowly
crept northwards to Florence.

These are from south of Rome, she'd say.
The next week—*from the Marches*.
Then *from Umbria*—then *Tuscany*.
We felt them rising, urgent as a flood.

Each day at supper, the new peas soloed
on our plates—tiny globes
dressed with flecks of rosy ham,
ambrosial to our tongues.

At last—late May—Lina sailed
into the dining room, platter held high
in triumph over her head: *"Piselli nostrani!"*
she announced, "Our very own peas!"

We bowed over our plates, we tasted.
Was anything ever so good?
The children hushed, dipping their spoons.
For ten days, we reveled.

Then the season was over. The tide
gone on to Bologna—Milano—Turin
—who knows? Flowing greenly
up into the passes, over the Alps.
In Florence, it was time for morels.

Juice

You write of this fall's bounty—
the grapes from your arbor
bursting their purple skins
and now your jelly-glasses lined up
glowing on the kitchen sill
like a row of votive lights...

October—was it six years ago?—
we sat under a *taverna*'s tattered arbor
awash in the foxy tang of grapes.
Wasps clung to the stained tablecloth,
dunked themselves headlong
into our cups of sweet Greek coffee,
their bodies pumping in frenzy.
Brushed off, they would rush back
to clamber recklessly
on the backs of our hands,
entangle themselves in our hair...

Reminded by your letter, I search
the stores in vain for Concord grapes—
thinking of the skin, how it
splits wide when you squeeze it,
emitting the whole fat grape,
translucent green and wet.
Thinking how it would be to plunge
like a wasp headfirst
into that slippery globe and probe
its tight little fist of seeds
—up to my waist, up to my
greedy heart in all that juice.

Scenario

That woman in the ratty
old fur coat is not me—I

wouldn't wear the thing, and certainly
not in August. Or with bare feet.

This is my dream, though, and in it she
hurries away through icy corridors

in a hospital, or maybe, come to think
of it, an *insane asylum*—as one used

to call such places. And how crazy
is it after all to cover her bony body

with Grandma's fur coat and yet
put nothing at all on her naked feet?

What a sight! No wonder the white-coats
need to take a blood sample, check her out

before they send her down the hall
to the door behind which her therapist

sits, inscrutable as ever. He hands her
a prescription slip, dismissing

her without a word. *O foolish ghost:
you are not me—and he, dead these*

many years—is not him. Merely a tenacious
tenant amongst a crowd of others:

parents and dogs, houses, landscapes,
nursemaids and lovers,

poised behind a door in the mind's
enormous motel, ready to live again.

Swimmers

In a hidden channel between the flats,
we anchor the skiff against a grassy bank,
shuck off our clothes
and slide into the current.
Salt water flows in from the sea,
cool and silky; the black mud underfoot,
thick with the soup of tides,
sucks at our ankles. We paddle,
talking, floating as the current carries us.

Ospreys wheel and cry overhead
and a pair of yellowlegs darts past,
heedless of our presence. A boat
motors up the main channel nearby
but we play unseen, twisting like otters.
Her worn-out knees, my stiff hips
make clumsy work of hauling
our wet bodies over the thwarts
back into the boat.

But when we've toweled off,
and sit drying in the last heat
of afternoon sun, these old breasts
and bellies, shoulders and thighs
glow as though lit from within.

Together

Old mule, my body—
you are the one
I tow along with me
down this unfamiliar path:
stubborn as ever,
you pick your way
on worn hooves,
hocks knocking together,
one eye gone milky,
whiskers sprouting
all over your chin.

Together we go on
plowing the one deep furrow
in a long field that tapers
from broad to narrow.
Moving steadily where
the going's easy, more slowly
among tussocks
and half-buried rocks.

At times it seems you
take the lead, at times it's me
that's pushing step by step
through the heavy loam,
the matted grasses.
And then, too, sometimes
we have to come to a halt—
when I need to admire
a grasshopper or when you
decide to stop and gaze
at some wonder only you
can see, hovering there
at the edge of the woods.

Lincoln Park Zoo

Off in one corner,
the solitary polar bear
is making a sort of backward somersault
in ice-green sheets of spray.   Down below,
through plate glass observation ports,
you see how he does it. Again.
Again. That tumbling circle, the amazing
bulk of him sailing by in his mantle
of bubbles, huge paws thrusting off.
The ecstasy of that creamy fur
as it billows past, revealing at belly's
root the neat rosette of his sex.
The priestly head is bowed in a nimbus
of foam. Eyes shut, he does not notice
us. Children, awestruck, then bored,
begin to bang on the glass. Parents'
cameras dangle: there's nothing here
for a snapshot. Nothing to watch except
compulsion's endless arc.
                        They leave.
The acrobat goes on with his ritual.
Working to get it right? Each turning
your try for the perfect dive? Or have you
become a prayer wheel, repeating
some mantra ice floes chant
into the polar darkness? There is no
ice here in your private ocean.
They gave you artful rocks, azure
lagoon, a black hatchway that leads
indoors. All night, I hold against my body
the curve of your body's journey.

Ode to the Porcupine

Just what was God
thinking, I wonder,
when he devised you
and set you free
up in the trees?
Solitary as the sloth,
with a face like a boot,
your passion is salt:
chewing the bark of conifers,
yellow teeth
sharp as machetes,
gnawing
sweaty shoes,
handles of tools
salty with human use,
sniffing out the liverwort,
the yellow water lily
and the rock-salted debris
along the highway.
Oh be careful,
dear stupid quill-pig!

Clumsy, and greedy too,
sometimes you over-reach
in search of a tasty twig,
to fall like a ripe apple
out of the tree,
to waddle forth
smelly as an old hermit,
your weak eyes
searching the dark world.
Only if disturbed
do you raise up
those fearsome weapons
with their barbed tips.

I celebrate you
because you are so much

like my own heart:
slow-moving, near-sighted
and like you wearing
an undercoat of silky down
beneath its armor
of rattling quills
so ready to bristle
with anger
or doubt, so slow
to recover.

Traveling...

how you always needed to look
into lit rooms—a kitchen at dusk, where
a family sits down to supper—or a backyard,
where a woman in a flowered housecoat
holds a hose over her geraniums
or a boy is throwing sticks for a black mutt.
Each story filtered through the dusty window,
the smudged mirror of your own face.

Even now, driving up a dirt road
and passing a sign, *For Sale—9 Acres,*
it starts again—thinking how you'd cut back
the sumac to free that stand of birches,
prune the ragged apple trees,
build yourself a house. There, yes,
by the ledge where the bracken grows.

Or glimpsing a white farmhouse
set well back from the road
with a lawn and two big maples,
you know how it would be to sit at dusk
on that porch, resting your bones
on an old striped-canvas-covered glider
that smells of citronella, dog and mildew,
a glass of iced tea in your hand,
watching cloud shadows cross the valley.

You would know the name of that mountain,
yes, know all its trails by heart
and remember the small cave—
there, where the granite outcrop
shows above the fringe of evergreens—
where, one summer years ago, you came upon
fresh bear scat and a rusted-out flashlight.

Here is the drawer where we keep candles
in case of a power failure, here is
the shoebox full of snapshots—

the wedding and last year's trip to Norway.
Down in the woods someone is working a chainsaw,
and the blue jays bounce from tree to tree, crying out.

IV

Half a Cloak

> *Saint Martin of Tours is often pictured on horseback,*
> *about to cut his cloak in half to give it to a beggar.*

The man stands on the traffic island as I drive past,
holding a handmade cardboard sign: *DISABLED VET*
SINGLE FATHER   SOBER   OUT OF WORK
in wobbly letters, a litany of disasters.
His brown hair flops, a cigarette hangs from his mouth.
No coat—in sneakers—he weaves through frozen slush
among the cars stopped at the red light,
holds out one hand and struggles to clamp the other
over one ear against the brutal wind.

Errands done, I go into Brine's Sporting Goods,
buy a fleece headband, a pair of Sherpa socks.
Will he still be there? I walk back to the crossing
where, yes, he's flapping his arms, limping back and forth
like a stork. Handing him the bag and the green
wool scarf I've been wearing. *Here—green for luck!* I say.
Green for money, he barks. *They stole my disability check!*
He looks in the bag, then wraps a bony arm around me.
I'd kiss you if you aren't married, he laughs.
Wear them! I say, like a parent. And walk away
in my down parka, my fur-lined boots.

Bad News...

when it arrives, looks much
like any other package left
at the door. Could be those jeans
from L.L. Bean—but you know better.

You want to open it right away.
You don't want to open it, ever.
But already it's giving off a smell
which will only get worse.

Unwrapped, in the light, it makes
an ugly sight: bigger even than expected,
the colors murky. The card says,
Nothing will ever be the same.

You carry the thing from room to room:
where to put it? You'll need to rearrange
the furniture, give some things away—
maybe even that picture you love.

You'll need to stop wondering
what visitors will think. In a few months
or years, you and this thing will have
come to a kind of agreement.

Some nights you will be able to fall asleep
without grief. Some mornings, wake up,
read the headlines, make the coffee
before you remember.

Will it always hurt this much? *Yes.*
Or maybe *No*. It will become one
of the ten thousand griefs each of us
is given. And the ten thousand joys.

Compassion

after the shootings at Virginia Tech. April, 2007

This is for you, Kwan Yin or Avalokiteshvara,
however you are called, that sits
with one arm draped across a knee,
one foot touching down onto
our human earth. Listen:
the mothers, the fathers are crying
and the crying goes on and it will not stop:
the father of the murdered girl who loved horses
and wanted to become a veterinarian,
the mother of the silent boy
who took up a gun to speak for his anguish:
she weeps for what he could not utter.
I tell you their cries require answers
that have not yet come into being.
On the evening news
they're showing a 20-year-old
soldier with brain damage trying to learn again
to pronounce the name of his wife,
they are showing the latest images:
refugees in Darfur: the children's legs
brittle and black as the stalks of burnt trees,
old men hunkered like insects in the dust.
Then comes the weekly Honor Roll,
the names, the ages—18, 22, 19—
and the places they came from:
Valdosta, Chisum, Red Lodge, Slidell...

Compassion is said to be
a trembling of the heart
in the face of suffering...
You are poised with your right hand
reaching out always, your left foot stepping
down always into the mess of our existence.
Show us how to bear this endless weeping.
For you have seen it all, tirelessly borne witness
to our confusion and blindness,

our griefs and rages—and witnessed, too,
our wish to shut it all out.
Can't I just go out to shop for a new toaster,
browse in the bookstore? Can't I just plant
another bed of daylilies next to the fence
and write a check to Amnesty International?

What I need to know is this:
after we turn off the TV
where does that stream of images go?
Is the ether polluted with suffering the way
the atmosphere is filled with carbon dioxide?
And if so tell me, how do you,
Compassionate One that you are,
go on breathing?

Imagining the Muse

after Brancusi

Sleek as a cosmic egg
that burnished copper head
lies balanced on one cheek:

three waves for hair
two strokes for eyelids
mouth like a hyphen

Perfectly asleep, she dreams
us watching her repose:
dreams our nervous hands

our maps and lovers—
grass—the way light
touches the skin of the lake

the ring you lost—the words
you know but can't pronounce—
the road they said you couldn't miss.

Yet isn't she also the one
who likes to appear at the end of the feast
with a tray full of paper cranes?

And the guest who arrives one icy night
hours later than expected
with a feather boa, old red suitcase

and mismatched sandals? Or rushing past
in the rain in a limousine, the one who
flings you a bundle from the window:

unrolling the cloth, you discover
the disjointed parts of a doll—
jumble of fragile bones
and no instructions.

The Sign

He has never known the shape of it
does it look like a hand or a name
or the tracks of some animal, does it stay
the same or change the way clouds do
into shapes like letters and hands

Sometimes he fingers the scar
and thinks it must resemble
a lightning-mark burnt into a log
or the odd patterns left after a flood
in the drying mud of the courtyard

He used to try to see himself
in the green surface of the water-jar
tried secretly to find his face
in the glossy bottom of his bowl
in the flat bright eye of a child

At first it would ache at night
now when he wakes he feels it tingle
as it awakens too and stirs
like a drowsy snake that moves
in a dry summer field

It was years before he understood
that it kept him safer than any weapon
years when he let his hair grow long
wore his head-cloth knotted low
and went by a different name

Now Cain goes bareheaded on market day
barters his fagot of brushwood
for a measure of oil or salt
nobody bothers to stare at this grizzled
man with the mark on his forehead

They have forgotten his story:
he is no more remarkable
than the woman with the missing thumbs
the blinded mule tied to the millstone

His mark has grown into him the way
a nail grows into the heart of a tree

The Prince Who Married a Frog

When the King my father got tired
of waiting for us to find brides,
got bored with ambassadors offering
portraits of wellborn girls,
he roared: *Enough! Let each of my sons
shoot his best arrow into the blue.
Where it alights, there in that courtyard
he must find him a wife.
And be done!*
                Sergei, the eldest,
went first. His arrow flew like a hawk
over two counties to fall
smack at the feet of a princess—
long yellow braids, sixteen,
fat as butter.
                Then Kostya the Clever
took aim. He winged his shaft straight up—
so high it must fall back nearby
onto familiar ground—
where the Duke's tall daughter
was just then mounting her mare.
Lucky old Kostya...
                My turn:
the bow felt heavy as stone.
A swan flapped past as I drew.
My shot went wobbling into the swamp—
from which hopped forth
a frog, arrow clamped fast
in her jaws. She dropped it
right at my feet, sat back on her rump
waiting for praise.

O how they laughed—the brothers, courtiers,
grooms—the very kitchen-maids
could barely hide their sniggers.
Father, enraged, stuck to his edict.
At the wedding, I put on a brave face,
hid my disgust until the farce was over.

That night, in the marriage bed
I found at my side a girl
with silken limbs, hair the color
of heron's wing. Her frog skin
hung on a peg behind the door.
I used to waken at dawn
to watch her mending my cloak,
to smell the fresh bread baking...

Still, they would joke over ale-pots
how I was so foul I'd sleep with a frog,
how my clothes always stank of damp,
how my get would be born
with pop-eyes and web-feet.
My love saw the hurt, offered at last
to show her human form
just once to the world.
                You know
the rest: at Michaelmas Ball
the whole kingdom amazed
at her grace, the shimmering darts
of her speech, her wise unusual face.
At midnight, as she danced
in a circle of tranced admirers,
I ran to the house, grabbed frog skin
and hurled it into the fire.
It flared up green, a rush of flame
like a squall tearing through reeds.

O, I didn't know
the shape of her need...
Weeping, she left me. Now I search
through all the swamps of the world.
And every human face
croaks out at me
its dumb reproach.

Prospero, Departing

> *"...the isle is full of noises"*
> —The Tempest

His spells dissolved, the air
at last allowed to be
only air

His staff changed to tree fern,
cape a carpet of black iguanas
sunning

This island becomes us now:
each cave rehearses its own
rumble

the small volcanoes croon
to one another all night like
owls

Lizard and dove and tortoise,
we were ancient before these
strangers

Caliban was root and mud then,
Ariel a taste of sea mist,
mere salt

Before she grew tall, Miranda
could track us where we hid,
found

footprint in moss, lichen
scribble on rock, a signal
guessed

She's gone now into humankind,
her dreamings lost: the island
sings itself

Miranda, Waking

Turning over in the wide bed,
you hear something rumble
over beyond the bay:
Is that Vesuvius? you wonder,
*And do the farmers, snug
in their stone huts on the mountainside,
hear it too? The fisher-folk, dozing
under their upturned boats—
do they smell a coming storm?*

You remember how you rested
like an egg at the bottom of a deep nest,
your father's cave
wrapped in feathery darkness,
his candle the only star
you ever needed.

Beside you now
your husband stirs and twitches,
restless as a puppy. *Ferdinand,*
you whisper, touching his shoulder
to quiet him. You want to believe
he can keep you safe,
believe he will always be patient
when you stumble over court protocol,
always find your mangling
of his native tongue
adorable.

Your father made
a great wall of wonder
around you. Now you feel your toes
stretching out against the silken sheets,
longing for the kiss of wet sand,
the scrape of limpet-spotted rocks
where you ran barefoot with Ariel...

Who am I now? Distant roosters start
to answer one another. The hinges
of daybreak begin to turn.

Mt. Fuji Between the Waves
off the Coast of Kanagawa

That morning, Master, we hastened to the beach at dawn. It was very
   cold. In winter, there is much sickness, so only a few of us are able to
   go forth. Just three boats went out that day. Hunger, however, knows
   nothing of these matters and the fish do not take note of the
   fishermen. The air was so cold it cut like ice in the wash-bucket.
   Each man who owned a quilted coat made haste to put it on.

Beyond the Holy Mountain the sky was dark grey; over the sea
   it was pale as cold ashes. The sea itself was ink, black and
   ready and silent.

We launched out longboats, eight men at oars and the captain on the
   foredeck. For six hours we cast our nets. Never in all my days—
   and I am the oldest man in our village—have I seen such a run of
   fish! Then the wind began to blow from the North; the sea began
   to speak. Captains shouted back and forth between the boats,
   Should we turn back? Shall we go on? They could not agree.

The Holy Mountain watches us, lifting her white brow above a cloak
   of blue. One boat turns back and makes for shore. Waves cover it
   from sight; we do not see it again. The sky is a shining
   mirror, the wind speaks in a hundred tongues. Great claws of foam
   reach out from the peak of each wave. Our boats carve through the
   enormous swells. Leaning over the oars, we labor like ants that
   try to move a leaf through tall grass. We groan like women in child-
   birth. The steersmen cry out as each wave approaches. Their cries are
   lost in the howl of the seas.

A giant wave appears from the West. It reaches for us with a
   thousand arms, a thousand hands, a thousand mouths. The sea
   roars with hunger. Gobbets of foam as big as summer hailstones
   pelt down on our backs. Our lungs are breaking. The nets wash
   overboard.

Only for a moment do I stop to wipe the foam and salt from my eyes.
 In the distance, beneath a sky patterned rose and pale-grey
 like the kimono of a maiden, I behold Mt. Fuji, small as the
 little hill where the children go for firewood.

Master Hokusai, this is all I remember.

Carmelina

after Matisse

You sit facing us
mantled in sunlight,
sturdy and whole
as a loaf of new bread.
Shadows define
your body.
At your belly's center
the deep well of the navel
is a promise of plenty.

Like a beacon you glow against
the ochre of the wall,
the gray of an empty fireplace.
The artist is a red blotch
in the mirror,
trying to set down
on canvas this unabashed wonder—
no more wonderful to him, perhaps,
than the blue jug on the table,
no more sexual
than a bunch of tulips.

What is there to stare at?
remarks your gaze.
No odalisque or nymph,
you wear your nakedness
like a robe of clear water.

(If one dared touch that skin
or the heavy braid of hair
it would be like touching
the flank of a lioness.)

How do I learn this ease?
To drop the self—its shame,
its complicated appetites
and its lies,
as casually as you've dropped
that pink towel
across one thigh?

Still Life

Six apples on a platter
a rumpled napkin
and a tumbler—

alphabet of comfort:
the small Norman apples
with their dents and blemishes

like a troop of schoolchildren
repeating their lesson, saying
Red, saying *Round*

the way a bird at dusk
high in the trees chants
the only six notes it knows

in endless variation
reminding us we are
still alive, and home again

in the homeliness of apples
the blue folds of linen
the welcome glint of water

Joy

A wet leaf glints in the sun
a jay calls out in the woods

Coolness touches my face
for a moment: this edge of joy

how it comes and goes, teasing
like the edge of foam that rides

the beach ahead of each wave
to be swallowed with a sigh

into wet sand until the next one
rises, and the next

About the Author

Geraldine Zetzel grew up in New York, Switzerland, and Washington, D.C. and spent summers in Austria and Wyoming. Her career was in teaching, teacher training, and child advocacy. In addition to poetry, she is active at the Harvard Institute for Learning in Retirement and with Cambridge at Home, an organization for seniors who choose to stay put as they age. The author of two chapbooks, *Near Enough to Hear the Words* (Pudding House Publications) and *With Both Hands* (Finishing Line Press), she is a student of Buddhism and lives in Cambridge, MA.

Other Recent Titles from Mayapple Press:

Penelope Scambly Schott, *Six Lips*, 2010
    Paper, 88 pp, $15.95 plus s&h
    ISBN 978-0932412-843

Toni Mergentime Levi, *Watching Mother Disappear*, 2009
    Paper, 90 pp, $15.95 plus s&h
    ISBN 978-0932412-836

Conrad Hilberry and Jane Hilberry, *This Awkward Art*, 2009
    Paper, 58 pp, $13.95 plus s&h
    ISBN 978-0932412-829

Chris Green, *Epiphany School*, 2009
    Paper, 66 pp, $14.95 plus s&h
    ISBN 978-0932412-805

Mary Alexandra Agner, *The Doors of the Body*, 2009
    Paper, 36 pp, $12.95 plus s&h
    ISBN 978-0932412-799

Rhoda Stamell, *The Art of Ruin*, 2009
    Paper, 126 pp, $16.95 plus s&h
    ISBN 978-0932412-782

Marion Boyer, *The Clock of the Long Now*, 2009
    Paper, 88 pp, $15.95 plus s&h
    ISBN 978-0932412-775

Tim Mayo, *The Kingdom of Possibilities*, 2009
    Paper, 78 pp, $14.95 plus s&h
    ISBN 978-0932412-768

Allison Joseph, *Voice: Poems*, 2009
    Paper, 36 pp, $12.95 plus s&h
    ISBN 978-0932412-751

Josie Kearns, *The Theory of Everything*, 2009
    Paper, 86 pp, $14.95 plus s&h
    ISBN 978-0932412-744

Eleanor Lerman, *The Blonde on the Train*, 2009
    Paper, 164 pp, $16.95 plus s&h
    ISBN 978-0932412-737

Sophia Rivkin, *The Valise*, 2008
    Paper, 38 pp, $12.95 plus s&h
    ISBN 978-0932412-720

Alice George, *This Must Be the Place*, 2008
    Paper, 48 pp, $12.95 plus s&h
    ISBN 978-0932412-713

For a complete catalog of Mayapple Press publications, please visit our website at *www.mayapplepress.com*. Books can be ordered direct from our website with secure on-line payment using PayPal, or by mail (check or money order). Or order through your local bookseller.